I0528945

MORE THAN WORDS

Your Good Words Enhance the Direction of Your Life

Written by

SAMUEL ANDREWS

Quantum
Discovery
A LITERARY AGENCY

More Than Words
Copyright © 2023 by Samuel Andrews

ISBN
978-1-961601-73-4 (Paperback)
978-1-961601-74-1 (eBook)

More Than Words

"Your Good Words Enhance The Direction Of Your Life"

Based Upon True Stories
by Samuel Andrews

TABLE OF CONTENTS

INTRO

My name is Samuel and this is the story of my journey into finding my true self through the power of prayer, travel and words. From a young age I always felt restless and longing to explore and discover more about the world and myself. It wasn't until I started actively incorporating prayer into my daily routine and taking the leap to travel to new places that I was able to start on the path to self discovery truly.

Through the highs and lows of my travels and the moments of quiet contemplation and prayer I have learned the importance of being open to new experiences and listening to the comfort and guidance of God. These experiences have helped me shape into the person I am today and have given me a deep sense a purpose and direction.

In this book and the screen plays based on this book along with the true stories I will share the lessons I have learned and how the power of intentional words, prayer and travel has brought me closer to my true self and God.

So join me in this journey of self discovery and see the transformative power of prayer and travel in your own life.

Also the book discusses the power of prayer and traveling in locating oneself by speaking life giving words. We will discover how the act of prayer can bring us closer to our authentic selves and how travel can challenge and expand our understanding of the world and ourselves through the stories of individuals who have who have undergone transformative journeys both inward and outward.

The lessons that may be learned from these pages will speak to the traveler that resides in every one of us regardless of how much or little we have travelled in the past. We will learn how to access our own inner knowledge and direction via the power of prayer as well as how to break out from our comfort zones and get fresh views through traveling. Find how out the power of prayer and travel may bring you to your authentic self by joining us on this journey of self discovery.

CHAPTER ONE
SPEAK, PLAN AND GO

I have learned over the years that there is a certain power in how we speak about the things we want. The power of speaking things into existence also known as the law of attraction. It is the belief that we can manifest our desires and goals through the power of our thoughts and words. The Bible says life and death are in the power of the tongue. Whatever we say we live from it. This idea is based on the idea that our thoughts and words have powerful energy that can attract experiences and circumstances into our lives good words can attract good things and bad words can attract negative outcomes.

This is not hocus pocus or as some preachers call mystic. This theory can be found in the Bible as many Biblical characters own words kept their lives stagnant or released the power of supernatural movement in their lives.

According to this belief when we become aware of our thoughts and words, we participate in what we want to see happen in our lives.

We send a message to the universe to bring those things into our reality. It is believed that by speaking these things into existence we can attract abundance success and great meaningful experiences.

Some people confuse the universe and God some people are afraid to use the word God because God has been so misrepresented at times by those who claim to represent him. The truth is God is the universe. God created the world and so when I'm talking about the universe I'm talking about God.

God created this universe, the multiverse, everything after and before and everything present. Our destiny has already been written and it's up to us to walk in it freely and in peace with no fear of outcome because we are confident in our Creator and our place.

MY PERSONAL EXPERIENCE

I would learn from this experience very well as an adult. While the law of attraction is a controversial topic there is little scientific evidence to support its effectiveness many people have claimed to have successfully manifested their desires through the power of positive thinking and speaking.

I always like to say that can do all things and endure through Christ who strengthens me. Some people believe that speaking such things into existence helps to create a mindset of abundance and positivity which can lead to an overall improvement in one's life.

Regardless of whether or not the law of attraction is truly effective. It is widely agreed that having a positive mindset and focusing on our goals and desires can be beneficial in helping us to achieve them. My source is the Bible so if there is a chance that speaking things into existence brings positivity in your life, there is no harm in giving it a try.

MY JOURNEY

I began to manifest certain things in my life when I decided to leave the states and live in Europe. I lived in Europe/ Germany for 11 years from 1992 to 2003 when I first came to Germany I was 27 and I only had a couple $100's in my pocket. I stayed at a friend's house. He let me stay with him for a few weeks. He also told me I had to get a job quickly so I was desperate.

I went on base and I found a job at the PX also known as the American commissary on the American base where Americans shop. It was the base where American soldiers and families lived and the jobs were reserved for American families who were serving but after going there a few times they gave me a job. While getting my hair cut at one of the barber shops on the base the barber asked me what I was doing there? I blurted out "I'm a singer "and he replied Oh really? before stating that he knew of a person forming a new group that could use my skills.

It was amazing because I had been hoping and believing something might work in my favor to start making music. He called the woman and told her that he had found a background singer for her choir that she was starting. I met with her and auditioned. After hearing my voice range she immediately offered me the job. Things were beginning to look up.

Starting in December of that same year, I was touring with Joan Faulkner. We went to many television stations in Germany and Tv networks like ZDF, RTL and Viva Tv in Cologne, Germany, Hamburg, Germany, Austria, Amsterdam and all over the place. Joan took me around and we had a great time singing. I met my best friend in Germany, Esther a girl around the same age as I was. She was from Kenya, Africa so we all had a great time. I learned perseverance and how to develop a fantastic work ethic from her and the other group members lead by Joan Faulkner.

CHAPTER TWO

WHAT IS IN YOUR HAND?

There is nothing quite like the joy of unexpectedly making a new friend. Weather it is through a chance encounter at a coffee shop a mutual connection or at a social gathering or even striking up a conversation with a stranger on the street. The experience of connecting with another person on a deeper level can be truly fulfilling and rewarding. **I look for, notice and acknowledge God in every situation** through out each day.

The excitement of getting to know someone new and learning about their interest, passions and experiences can be invigorating. It can bring new perspectives and insights into our own lives and as we build relationships with these unexpected new friends. We often find that they become an important valued part of our social circles enriching our lives in ways we could have never predicted. An open life and trust in God will lead you to more than you ever imagined.

I had the exquisite pleasure of meeting someone in the choir that was my friend and sister for years. Her name was Esther she was from Kenya she was both beautiful on the inside and outside. Her hair was beautifully braided even before it was a popular style.

We became friends from the very first day we met. We had such a great easygoing demeanor we stayed friends until she left the choir because she wanted to focus on raising her family. But my experience meeting Esther introduced me to other sister friends.

We would always laugh and share secrets. She was with me on the train when we went to Austria to do a show and on the way to the front the border guards got on the train.

That was about a few weeks before the European Union began and so the border guards would lose their jobs and there would be no more border guards. This was around 1999 or so when the Euro first began. I will go into this more in the movie, series and screenplays.

RACISM IN EUROPE

So we were on the train when the Austrian border guards arrived they saw this group of black people going to Austria and they stopped the train before having us removed. They took us into a room to interrogate us after inspecting our documents. We were told that our passports were fake. We were separated into different rooms and interrogated when it was my time to go in the officer attempted to interview me in German. I couldn't quite understand fully despite knowing a bit of the language so I had to wait for the interpreter to answer the his questions. The interrogator finally gave up then they all gave up and they let us go. We made it to our show on time but it was an embarrassing situation for us.

Racism is a significant problem in Europe as it is in many other parts of the world. It manifests in many forms including discrimination, prejudice and violence against individuals or groups based on their perceived race or ethnicity. In our case we were all perceived to be African not Americans. The African passport to them was not as powerful as the American passport. Most of our members passports were American but we were harassed anyway.

Many factors contribute to racism in Europe. One is the legacy of colonialism which is European based, in which the powers exerted control over and exploited the resources of other countries and their peoples for centuries. This history has lasting effects on relationships between European countries and the countries that were colonized as well as within European societies.

Another factor is the increasing diversity of European societies has more and more people from various racial and ethnic backgrounds that have migrated to or been born in European countries. Some people may feel threatened or uncomfortable with this diversity leading them to express racist attitudes and behaviors.

Some societal structures and systems perpetuate racism in Europe such as education systems that fail to adequately address and confront the history of colonialism and its impact or economic systems that disproportionately benefits certain racial ethnic groups over others.

Efforts to combat racism in Europe include education and awareness campaigns initiatives to promote diversity and inclusion and policy changes to address and rectify the effects of historical and ongoing discrimination.

It is an ongoing challenge but it is crucial to address to create more equitable and just societies.

CONTINUING TO MOVE FORWARD

It was also an uncomfortable situation for Austria because of those border guards. Later both Esther and I were sent a letter with an apology. I wish I had kept that letter but they apologized for the antics of their guards who are about to lose their jobs anyway because of the coming European Union.

Experiencing injustice can be a difficult and traumatic experience. It can be challenging to know how to move forward. I decided to forgive and move forward. I decided not to hold grudges.

My time in Europe taught me a few lessons. One was to move past the looks, racism and other things I experience as back then as I do now- I choose blessings not curses. I choose forgiveness. I choose life not death. We all have a choice. We can all choose. I choose life.

SEEK FRIENDS.

It can be helpful to talk about your experience with someone you trust, whether a friend, family member or therapist finding a supportive network of people who can listen and offer emotional support and consistent prayer can be invaluable. Take care of yourself make sure to prioritize self-care such as getting enough sleep, eating well and finding ways to relax and recharge.

Engaging in activities that bring you joy and a sense of purpose can also be helpful. Seek justice if you feel you have experienced injustice. Consider seeking legal or other recourse. This may not always be possible or appropriate but it can be a way to hold those responsible.

Try and prevent similar injustices from happening to others. It can be difficult to find meaning in difficult experiences but try to find a way to make sense of what happened and how it affected you. It can be helpful and a way to move forward. This might involve finding ways to advocate for change or supporting others who have experienced similar injustices.

PRACTICE FORGIVENESS

These doesn't mean forgetting what happened or condoning the injustice you've experienced but it can be a way to release the anger and bitterness that can hold you back if not internally addressed in a healthy manner leading to release.

Allow your self to move forward only after you have correctly addressed your feelings about the issue.

It's important to remember that healing and moving forward after experiencing injustice is a process that will take time. It's OK to take things one step at a time.

Be kind to yourself as you navigate your journey.

CHAPTER THREE
WHAT IS UNIQUE ABOUT YOU?

I made the journey to step out in faith and by the grace of God I was well taken care of. I had a very precious family. They took me under their wing when I lived in Germany. They were a great German family and they had a great furniture company called Meinzer Moble.

The father had been so successful he had billboards all over the country. The father had also spent time in the war.

He would try to tell me stories of his time as a prisoner as a German soldier. He wasn't a Nazi but he was in the military around the war and was taken prisoner by the Russians.

This family was very dear to me.

Every Christmas they invited me to their house and gave me Christmas dinner. This continued for years. The mother Doris would bake a large batch of cookies with all colors and shapes. After we ate the main dinner the older people would go for a long walk in the snow. They would walk us all around the town in deep snow. This became a yearly tradition. The mother Doris lived to be in her 90's and the father lived close to be 100 years old. They gave me unconditional love despite me being from a different culture and a different race.

They welcomed me as a member of their family even allowing me to spend more time with them and their nieces and nephews. They let me teach them African American songs-gospel songs and the songs I grew up listening to in America-from my church. I go into this more in the movie version on this book. The Germans would learn these songs quickly. It was such a wonderful time exchanging cultures with no holds barred and unconditional love being exchanged.

What is unique about your life?

What is not typical about you that can help others? The answer is part of your calling.

THE JOY OF A NEW FAMILY

It can be a wonderful feeling to be accepted as a part of a new family by people who are essentially strangers and from another culture. Being welcomed into a new group of people and feeling like you belong can be a joyous, affirming and deeply fulfilling experience.

A few things contribute to this feeling of joy and acceptance. Finding new relationships can create a new sense of belonging for those who have been hurt or come from broken families.

We can feel like we're part of a new family. It can give us a sense of belonging and connection to others that can be deeply meaningful and fulfilling. There is something special about feeling accepted by a different culture it creates a feeling of being valued.

When people accept us into their family it can be a validation of our worth and value as a person. This can be especially meaningful if we have struggled to find acceptance in other areas of our lives.

Meeting this family also created a powerful sense of connection for me. Being part of a family even a group of strangers in a different country can give us a sense of connection to others and a feeling of being a part of something larger than ourselves.

I found my new family a new source of support and strength. This is important for all of us. Having a sense of family can provide us with support and care during difficult times. It can be comforting to know that there are people who will be there for us and have our back. Ultimately the joy of being accepted as family by strangers comes from the sense of connection belonging.

It can be a wonderful and enriching experience that brings happiness and fulfillment to our lives. I know it did so for me and I currently try to pass this on to others who may have problems with their family because the human family is large and capable of loving everyone on this earth in a way that matters.

CHAPTER FOUR
CONFRONTING YOUR OBSTACLES.

I met a woman named Joan Faulkner. She was a lead singer and the founder of the group that hired me. I came to realize that she was a very popular singer in Germany at that time but even more than her singing she was a good hearted person. Her word was her bond if she spoke it, it happened. If she told you it would happen it would occur. If she had trouble making it happen, she still made it happen she showed good character and strength.

I had never met anyone that way who would do something for someone in need with no strings attached. She was just who she was. She was an honor to work with. She would do concerts by herself or without us. She was a working person and encouraged me to try outside projects in music and do other things then working with her. So I ended up doing a Bounty candy commercial with other singers and writing other songs and background singing jobs for other artists while I lived in Germany because she was secure and allowed her background singers to do outside projects.

She was secure in herself and secure with us, in letting us grow as human beings. She also predicted that I would lead group projects leading me to write screenplays. She called or help call more out of me before I even realized it myself.

Joan predicted that I would do other things that I didn't realize I had in me. I looked at her in shock when she would say these things.

Did she know the struggling person I was on the inside?

Maybe not. But I appreciated her calling those things which were not as they were which the Bible says we can do if we choose to believe.

Her character and her Godliness always has me reaching forward and encouraging others to reach forward even to this day.

SINGING FOR CELEBRITIES

One time we did a background singing job for Mariah Carey in Frankfurt, Germany. She had to get a black choir together to back her. So our choir combined with another choir and we sang background for Mariah Carey. That was great. I was on the same show on the ZDF network that Prince was on. I didn't meet Prince but he was there in the same Tv studio I was in. Also singer Bonnie Tyler and other American singers coming to Germany would be on the same show as we were. I was just a background singer experiencing so many great things. The sets of TV shows and set designs and cameras and retakes and all those things would have a major effect on me and my work today as a content writer for movies and series in Los Angeles.

This journey showed me that there is power behind belief. Speaking what we desire to come to pass and overcoming any giant that stands in our way by prayer will help.

Strong words, affirmations and belief in your God-given gifts will bring many great things to fruition in your life.

Prayer helps a lot no matter what situation one finds themselves. One should always consistently pray.

Keep a prayer in the back of your mind all day and on your heart during any situation to maintain hope and victory.

THE POWER OF THE SPOKEN WORD

All this because I use the power of the spoken word. Words are seeds. I believe that what we say and believe about ourselves will have an impact. As the Bible says; life and death are in the power of the tongue whatever we say, we live from it.

Many people may not understand or agree with this principle but I hope more people will slowly understand how powerful words are for their lives.

Words matter, negative words have negative impact positive words have positive impact what we say matters- what we say goes.

Talking about Germany led me to Germany while I was still in America. My friends thought I was crazy. They didn't believe me when I said I was going to Europe to live. When I later said I would put out a music CD my friends thought I was crazy but years later after hearing my music and seeing what I could accomplish they were amazed.

YOUR WORDS MATTER

Either way your words matter. What you think matters. What you say about yourself and those around you matters. Positive self speech or speaking kindly and positively to oneself can be incredibly important for overall well-being and happiness.

Negative self talk on the other hand can be harmful and can lead to feelings of low self esteem anxiety and depression.

Positive self speech benefits include improving self esteem. When we speak kindly to ourselves and to others we are more likely to have positive views of ourselves and our abilities, this can boost our self esteem and confidence.

Positive speech also reduces stress and anxiety. On the flip side negative self talk can contribute to stress and anxiety. But when we practice positive self speech we can reduce these negative emotions.

I was able to self promote motivation and goal achievement from within. Positive self speech can help us believe in ourselves and our ability to achieve our goals- increasing our motivation and drive to succeed.

Learning how to verbalize and actualize positivity can improve your mental health. Positive self speech can help to improve your overall mental health by reducing negative emotions and promoting a more positive outlook overall. Positive self speech is an important tool for improving our mental health and emotional well-being. It takes time and practice to develop but it can have a powerful impact on our lives.

CHAPTER FIVE
MEETING THE CONDITIONS

I was born in Tacoma, Washington. Tacoma is about an hour or less from Seattle. I was born in a hospital named Saint Joseph's hospital in Tacoma, Washington which had this reputation as a stinky little town because it was next to another small town called Fife that had a wood mill and it brought a foul smell when the water and the wind hit the city.

Every so often there would be a stinky smell in Tacoma and so they called it the Tacoma aroma.

Anyway I was born in Tacoma WA and was the first son of my father and my mother. They were swamped and busy with the children that came after me. They were good parents.

I came from a large family my mother gave birth to 14 children so I was responsible along with my other older brothers and sisters for taking care of the younger brothers and sisters.

I went to school right down the street from home at Stanley elementary school and then to Wilson high school. I was a terrible student because of my inability to focus or concentrate. I only really started getting myself together when I was 18.

I left home because I wasn't going to graduate high school and I went to Job Corps a government training program in the United States. It was a lifesaver for me because I was able to get my GED and work and learn a trade and from there I went to Broadcasting School in Portland, OR at that time it was called National Broadcasting School I was timid but it was perfect for me.

I remember when I went to National Broadcasting School. I wasn't as outgoing and I had terrible self esteem issues I thought I was smaller than I was.

Fast forward to my graduation from National Broadcasting School. I remember when they handed me my diploma the man that handed it to me was just as surprised as I was that I graduated. He was shaking his head while he handed me my diploma. Some friends that attended from church were also surprised that I made it. My friends from the church and the main representatives Victor and Roxanne a white couple came to the graduation ceremony and stood in for my parents. It was a great time.

In my screenplay, I tell the story of how Victor taught me about gun safety and my other great experiences with that fine couple.

STARTING MY CAREER

From there I went on to a radio station. I was doing an internship there while I was studying as well and they hired me. The program director told me I was hired because I was an African American which would have offended many people but that was my way in and I have no shame concerning why I was hired.

I've since adjusted my views on affirmative action and I think it was a very nice gift from America to African Americans but I do not believe that gift should last forever.

I worked at KPDQ Portland, OR while it was a Christian format for three years. I started working on call then I started working in the overnight shift. I used to fall asleep during the overnight shift. The phones would ring and wake me up and I would get back to work. I struggled with dead air or not having anything to say on the air for a few moments—this happens during development. After a few times falling asleep during the overnight shift I could have been fired but they didn't fire me. I switched to the swing shift leaving the midnight shift. Working 5:00 PM to 11:00 PM, I was honored that they thought that the people listening in the evenings would enjoy me. I had a chance to introduce BB and CC Winans who were popular at that time. I thought I was such a big shot for introducing them to a concert because I worked at the local station. I was so sure that it was the best thing that could ever happen to me.

CONTENT, BUT NOT HAPPY

During this time I felt so confident it wore off so I did not enjoy my job. I'm an introverted person and so that job caused me to be extroverted person so inside I wasn't that happy. But I did learn a lot there like writing copy for commercials, we had to write a copy very quickly. I wrote public service announcements before I would have to go in and record them immediately so I learned fast-paced work recording and working under pressure. I also learned a lot of things about radio. My favorite thing was engineering talk shows so I didn't have to speak we had a famous talk show host there. I had to engineer his show. To engineer his program was fantastic. I enjoyed the atmosphere there but I soon lost interest in it and so that's when I left.

STEPPING OUT IN FAITH

This is what prompted me to decide I will go to Europe and that's where my trip to Europe starts. I started talking to my friends and colleagues about Europe and how I wanted to go there and live there everyone around me didn't think that I was serious. They didn't take me that seriously. Some people even thought I had mental issues and that I was talking crazy but I knew about the power of words. Because I had heard somewhere that if you speak something and believe it you can have it. That's also in the Bible.

I've heard people who weren't Christians to do it. Words are powerful. Words have meaning. And words have repercussions. No matter what you believe.

I believe the things that we are willing to speak out loud can be a guide for discovering our life's purpose and I was very sure as well about the power of the tongue.

I know the power of words can hurt or they can heal so when I spoke about my desires I also began to save up enough money and I got a passport to go to Europe at the time you could go to Europe without a visa you cannot do that anymore this was 1992. It was election year so I voted before getting on a plane to go to Europe.

Moving there was one of the best decisions I had ever made for the next nine years I toured all over Europe and all over German, Amsterdam, Austria appearing on television shows in Germany, Austria and Holland it was amazing. So fast forward to 1996 I decided I wanted to have my own CD. CD's were still the thing there. People were starting to download music but it wasn't as slmple as it is now.

During that time I met a man on a train we were talking and he asked me where I was from and I said I from Tacoma, WA he replied hey I'm from Tacoma WA too! I asked him what are you doing here? He responded that he was married to a German woman working for a business man who had multiple ventures in Frankfurt.

He added that his boss was starting record label and I can take you over to meet him on Monday. Just like that I went and met his boss that next Monday.

Long story short I would receive a record deal within a few days of the meeting. Being a musician with a record deal challenged me in many ways. During a video shoot I froze. During the video and I wasn't prepared but despite obstacles I knew I was on the right track.

This is a reminder; You may have the opportunity you want but if you have not prepared for the opportunity it can be easy to lose it. The day after the video shoot. I was disappointed. I went home and got into my bed and I stayed there for three days. I was so embarrassed that I bombed on the video shoot. I got a call a few days later from a friend of someone who was on that set, he asked me if I wanted to shoot another video- he asked me if I wanted another shot.

I said yes!

I did another video called Higher on a music Vinyl EP for Interscope Music. It was there that I was able to redeem myself.

FOLLOWING YOUR DREAMS

Following your dreams can be a challenging and rewarding journey and setbacks are inevitable. They are a part of the process. It can be easy to get discouraged when things don't go as planned but it is important to remember that setbacks are a natural part and a normal part of any journey. The key is not to let them hold you back but rather to use setbacks as an opportunity to learn grow and persevere.

One way to overcome setbacks is to keep things in perspective. It can be helpful to remind yourself that setbacks are normal and are an expected part of the process that they don't define your worth or abilities. It's also important to focus on the progress you have made rather than dwelling on the setbacks.

Another way to move forward despite setbacks is to stay resilient and adaptable. This means being willing to try new approaches and ideas, when the other idea doesn't go as planned and being open to learning from your mistakes. It can be helpful to seek out the support of others whether it's friends family mentors and a supportive community, it's important to choose the right mentor.

Someone who's never managed before or cannot manage their own life should not be used as your manager. A mentor must come from a successful avenue. From their own life you must be able to see light, goodness and results. Don't be so desperate that you choose someone from the dark to lead you to the light.

A mentor must be accomplished in something consistently and able to support you and their life successfully plus have a qualified history.

Ultimately the key to following your dreams despite setbacks is to stay focused on your goals but also to be flexible and open to new possibilities.

It may not always be easy but with perseverance determination and a positive attitude you can overcome any setbacks and achieve your dreams. I will go into more details during the movie version based my books.

CHAPTER SIX
BECOMING BETTER

So there I was in Germany working living and traveling and seeing all over the country of Germany and parts of Europe. I remember visiting Malta and seeing all the rocks where the apostle Paul's ship was wrecked.

Malta is a separate country from Germany mind you but I was able to travel to many other countries while in Germany. I've counted 19 countries that I travel to while living in Germany. Malta stood out. I went there because it was December and I thought Malta would be warm in the winter but it wasn't.

On New Year's Eve in Malta I got the worst toothache, I mean agonizing toothache. So on New Year's Eve 1999 I had to get my teeth pulled in a foreign country. It wasn't that scary because I was happy to have my tooth out. It was awful but things happened and I persevered.

I cannot stress enough the importance of determination. Being determined opened my life to so many blessings that it was hard to keep count. Such as singing, I was a good singer but not great but being good opened the door for me to learn and perform in Germany with other good singers.

I was good enough for background singing even though I've heard that it's better to have a background singer behind you that is better than you or it's good for a background singer to be better than the lead singer so the lead singer feels supported. I needed to be seen because I didn't feel like I was seen before. I wanted to be heard because I thought In my own head I was considered invisible. Many people feel that way perhaps you have felt that way.

Germany and this opportunity gave me a chance to be seen and heard like never before.

But I had to be a team player with other group members. I had to learn to compromise I had to learn to show up on time and not argue with the group's leader.

Many people stand their own way by not learning to listen and by not compromising or not being grateful for the moment and opportunity.

They try to stretch beyond their ability by arguing with leadership and becoming impossible to work with.

I don't believe human beings can be replaced but I can sometimes think another person can be recalled.

We are called to get along.

The Bible even tells us to do things without murmuring and complaining it took me a while to learn this but once I learned it I became an asset to where ever I went.

As now I am an asset to writing staff and an asset to my producers an asset to sets because I realize all great efforts are collaborative.

For example I could not write this book without the project manager or my literary agent. My literary agent has special talents that only belong to him. He loves people. He loves stories. He loves sharing stories. He plays an important role in my success.

I have to be able to understand the value of each person on my team and when I'm on the team I have to understand my own value within my role.

I am not the most talented person that you will meet. I'm not the most educated person that you will meet. But I'm the kind of person that will go for it and because I go for it a lot of people are shocked at what I come up with.

Every human being has this and more within them.

In 1996 I did the CD titled We Don't Stop.

I did a video and I was still working with Joan Faulkner I had the opportunity to see an awesome group of female singers. They were trending at the time they were called the Weather Girls and they were performing and they had really tight act.

They were big bold black women before it was trending to be big and black. They were unashamed you might remember their song; It's Raining Men.

So I went behind the scenes of the set of their show they were so kind. I showed them my CD and they replied good for you baby they were so encouraging to me.

One of their background singers had the greatest falsetto voices I ever heard, but he also had a drug problem behind the scenes. After the show he would smoke cocaine. It was tough because he had to perform every night and he received such a rush from the audience but afterward in his private time he would smoke this drug because he was looking for the same feeling he received from the audience every night.

Many artists go through this and so he at that time never admitted that problem. We need to admit our problems before we can begin to solve them.

Germany is only the size of Texas but you can do different things there that you couldn't do in America.

I did so. I went there and decided I wanted to do something artistically further that I ever had done before. You can meet your goals too. If you remember that your words have power.

I found a record label in Frankfurt Germany I wanted to go there myself but I needed an agent.

I didn't have an agent at that time. So I decided to go to the label alone. They were very kind to me as I sat in the lobby alone.

I would go there often and just sit in the lobby I would sit in the lobby day after day waiting to speak to someone about my vision.

In the record labels lobby I would sit and wait, and everybody would just come and go and not talk to me and look at me sitting on the green sofa with a smile on my face.

While in the lobby one day the receptionist told me directly " You know they're swamped"– they don't see many people from the street and I said that's OK maybe they'll see me one day. I must have gone there about six or seven times.

The owner of the label Pascal was the owner and founder of the Electrolux Music label in Offenbach, Germany. That type of electronic house music was very big at that time. The name of the label was called Electrolux. In America Electrolux was also a vacuum cleaner name but it Offenbach, Germany it was record label go figure.

So I just would hang out at the label until one day Pascal came over and he saw me and he says come on in and from then on I had an EP.

He would let me sit around with him and try different things until I had my first EP with the label. Pascal introduced me to someone named Peter from the group Freshmoods. He asked me if I would guest on an LP produced by him. Of course I said yes. We recorded a song called Price/ Find My Home it became very popular and was remixed very many times.

This song was a blessing for me. It opened up doors for me to be interviewed in Frankfurt by writers and it also provided financial help and even now residuals.

I bring this up so you can realize that some of the smallest things that we do in life can become huge and sometimes it's safe to keep your dream on the inside so other people who have given up on their dreams don't attempt to squash your dream.

Americans constitution says everyone has the right to life, liberty and the pursuit of happiness. My travels taught me that other countries also have humans who want to pursue happiness. What may be small to someone else will be considered large by you and vice versa.

We should not step on other people's dreams as we don't want someone to step on your own dream that could could be something that's very small that can grow into something large or something that is very satisfying to you and your purpose.

CHAPTER SEVEN
LOVE GOD AND TAKE RISK

It is possible to have a life changing and enlightening experience through the process of discovering oneself through travel and faith. We can expand our horizons and gain a fresh insight and perspective on the world by visiting unfamiliar locations and engaging in activities associated with a variety of cultures doing our travels.

At the same time faith has the potential to bestow upon us adherence a sense of purpose and connection to something that is more significant then themselves. A combination of travel and religious practice can offer a one-of-a-kind chance for individual development and discovery of oneself.

One of the ways in which travel can assist us in discovering who we are, is by the opening our minds to new concepts and providing us with fresh experiences. When we remove ourselves from our visual environment and immerse ourselves in the culture of another country we are compelled to examine the presumptions and beliefs that we bring with us.

It is possible for us to come across alternative ways of thinking and living that present a challenge to our perception of the world and the role that we play in it. This at times can be confusing but it can also be tremendously enriching because it enables us to see things from a different perspective and to challenge our own beliefs and values although it can be disconcerting at times it can also be quite enriching.

I personally have learned and grown from my travels. Sometimes even within the United States. Travelling from Portland OR to Utah was a shock to my system and a growth to my person. Travelling from Washington State to Georgia was a shock to my system and a growth to my person. Travelling from one neighborhood to another in safety and in peace can also expand one's views on the world.

Travel does not have to be across a border or boundary, it can be within a new person from another culture with an open mind and a desire to connect and grow.

Although new approaches from different cultures can be disconcerting at times it can also be quite enriching. On the other hand travelling can also present us with new possibilities of trying new things and expanding our comfort zones by forcing us to go to new places.

This can be especially true when we travel by ourselves since it compels us not only to rely on ourselves and to make choices based on our own judgment.

The development and self assurance together with identification of one's own qualities and advantages can be significantly facilitated by proper travel.

Finding oneself can be greatly aided by the practice of one's faith. A sense of connection to something that is more important than one self can be achieved via the practice of faith. Whether through prayer meditation or involvement in religious organizations.

It has the potential to bestow upon us a feeling of direction and purpose in our lives as well as a sense of significance and renewal in our daily lives.

In my upcoming movie based on this book I will dive into more stories based on my 11 years in Germany.

As an African American male I learned to identify and to relate to people outside of my culture and outside of English. I learned also to speak German but I also learned to understand German. I also learned and to understand other cultures such as Italy, Spain, France, and Holland. I was very moved by Romania. I was very excited to visit Austria even though we had problems there. And I was very satisfied when I visited Switzerland.

Connecting with other humans is the goal that we are here for on earth and coupled with faith in God and his creation we are challenged to understand and to see other people in ourselves.

Faith can also provide obstacles that force us to reflect on our identities and the things in which we place our faith. It might prompt us to contemplate our beliefs and priorities as well. We may question how we want to spend our lives which is a useful question. Some have their faith in wrong things in my view but I cannot tell you what to put your faith in except I would encourage you to put your faith in God which is the tried and true. Put your faith in the one that created you. In that safety your destiny is secure.

In the safety of the knowledge of your creator your purpose becomes clear. You become relaxed and more steel in the moment.

In time you become less competitive with other humans and more secure in who you are within the universe that God created for you.

Life will still be challenging but it has the potential to be extremely gratifying since it assists us in inoculating our own ideas and then leading a life that is genuine and meaningful in general. Traveling and having faith can be extremely useful tools for discovering one's true self. They have the potential to expose us to novel experiences and points of view as well as prompt us to consider our identities and the things in which we put our faith.

The Bible says all we need to have is a muster seed of faith which is a small amount of faith. A speck of a sand of faith and with that we can move a mountain. With that spec or sand grain of faith-that's just a tiny bit of faith- we can move mountains. This information is encouraging to me because I didn't have to believe a lot in my dreams and goals I just had to believe.

Faith also provides a feeling of connection and purpose and support. It assist us in navigating the highs and lows of life and living in a manner that is authentic to who we are as God's creation.

It is your right not to believe in anything or to believe in whatever you want but whatever you do travel, go past your comfort zone, go past your circle,your click, your group and your organization. Don't be the person that stays in the same

place their whole life without reaching out to another human. Don't be afraid to look at situations that affect others more than yourself. Lets not be afraid to grow and lets not be afraid to live.